The Artistry of God

DEVOTIONAL BEACH WALKS TO INSPIRE YOUR SOUL

Rebecca S. Parkinson

www.nature-reflections.com

Cover & interior design by Typewriter Creative Co.
All artwork by Kay Withington.

ISBN 979-8-9855962-0-5 (Paperback, color)
ISBN 979-8-9855962-1-2 (Paperback, black & white)
ISBN 979-8-9855962-2-9 (eBook)

Dedication

To Readers
Who search for solace, comfort, and joy.

To Mr. Fred Rogers
Who now knows.

To
The Lord Jesus Christ
Who spoke this book into being.

Grateful Thanks

I have always enjoyed reading a book's acknowledgment section because it shows how the hand of God works. So many people lent a hand, encouraged, held me accountable, prayed, and most of all didn't give up on me or the Lord.

With that in mind, I would like to give special thanks to the people who read the first edition of this book and shared it with their friends. Your comments on how the words ministered to you and others made my heart happy.

I would especially like to thank my friend Kay Withington. She is not only a great artist but also a dear friend for helping paint my words into watercolor illustrations. And to her husband, Kent, who meticulously prepared the artwork for the publisher. My gratitude also goes to Cyndee Ownbey for sending me to Taryn Nergaard and Sara Ward at Typewriter Creative Co. and for all the advice, creativity, and effort they put into making this book happen.

Many of my writing and reading friends have encouraged me along the way. Book signings are a great way to chat with readers. I'm thankful for Debbie Bruning for hosting me in her home. Donna Tuthill has been my encourager and personal publicity agent.

And finally, this book is a testimony of how God has His way, how He is involved in the particulars of our lives—in books, writers, and publishers. If I've forgotten you, know that you are still part of God's work and always part of my heart.

Soli Deo Gloria

Table of Contents

Introduction

I never intended to write a book about Nantucket. But God's plans and purposes are often different than ours and remain a mystery until revealed. These pages are a compilation of what the Lord spoke to me as I wandered along familiar paths that crisscross the island's marshes, moors, and beaches. And often, even in trying to apply my editor's red pen, His Spirit pushed back against me. I have found this true in other writing that He has given to me. And ultimately, this is a better place to be, for the scripture says His word goes out and does not return to Him void but instead accomplishes His purposes. (Paraphrase Isaiah 55:11)

This island, a fragile outpost of glacial moraine and outwash plain, was formed long before my footprints marked its sandy dirt roads. There is an unspoiled beauty of Life here that takes you back to the moment of creation. I know of few places in the world where I have felt the presence of the Creator God so profoundly. On Nantucket, I find His Spirit compelling and more personal than any other place in the world.

Since I was first carried to Nantucket in my mother's womb and yearly breathed its fragrant air, it is not surprising that I would find such noble companionship here with the Lord who created it. It is also quite understandable that when tossed about by the emotional and physical storms of life, I have found healing on this island for my soul, body, and spirit.

So you see, having been rooted and established on this sandy barrier island, it is not surprising that my conversations with the Lord would yield teaching and comfort, not only to me but also to many that step foot here. Nantucket captures the heart in a way that no other place does. We cannot help but encounter the Creator here. And as a result, we may leave mentally and physically refreshed and changed in spirit.

Like a small boat that sets out on a journey, I hope the Lord you see and experience through these stories and word pictures will touch you. And that you would be drawn toward this great and majestic God who loves you in a personal way and longs for an intimate relationship with you. His *heart is set* on you. Listen quietly for His words as you read curled up in your favorite chair, walk along a quiet beach, or hear the wind as it caresses the pink mallows across the marshes. You will find Him here. My prayer is this: as you turn these pages and learn of our great God's character and love for you, that you will find the relationship you are looking for and the joy that never fades. Discover this beautiful island and give thanks to our great God for the incredible handiwork and care He has taken to leave us such a protected place of His presence and glory.

"Sing to the Lord a new song,
his praises from the ends of the earth,
you who go down to the sea,
and all that is in it, you islands,
and all who live in them."

ISAIAH 42:10

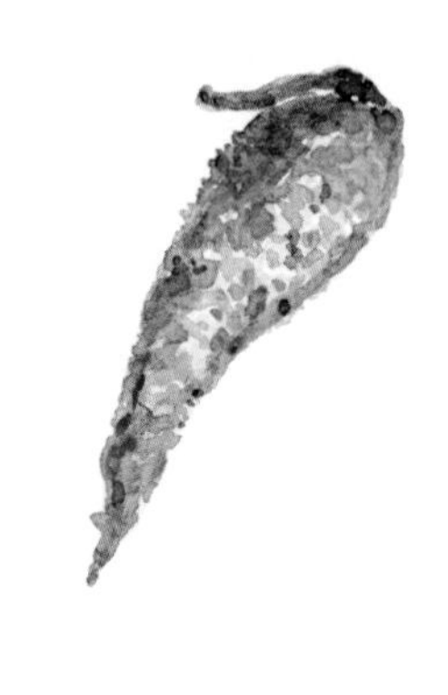

Chapter One

Restoration

"And the God of all grace, who called you to his eternal glory in Christ, after you have suffered a little while, will himself restore you and make you strong, firm and steadfast."

1 PETER 5:10

The ferry pulls away from its slip. As the thick hemp ropes lie curled up in neat piles, my troubles and responsibilities lie fallow until the ferry returns me to them.

The shore slips away, and I leave behind all that holds me. Mentally I begin to chart my course across that familiar passage. With impatient expectation, I await those few moments when the mainland is but a whisper of gray, and the island yet lies beyond the horizon. This is my cue to go forward to the bow and wait. Softly and mysteriously, Nantucket appears out of the fog like Brigadoon. Muskeget and Tuckernuck Islands, Great Point, and the white face of the dunes at Dionis welcome me home once more.

I belong here—like a seed carried on the wind, dropped from somewhere in the gray sky onto a high moor. There, reaching my feet into the soil, I put my face to the sun and find my home. Later, however, being uprooted and replanted, my soul longs for its home. Like the determination of the monarch butterflies and the homing instinct of the little birds that brave thousand-mile journeys, wherever I go, the soul of the island deep within beckons me back.

For many, there are other places. For me, all have lost their permanence, but one. Here I return to drink in the ever-present beauty and reflect on the intricacy of our Creator, His "invisible qualities—his eternal power and divine nature . . . being understood from what has been made, so that people are without excuse." (Romans 1:20). Nowhere is my spirit at peace except here. Nowhere is home except Nantucket.

Later, standing at the high-water mark on the beach, the soft sand slips through my toes like an hourglass. The wind touches my cheeks, and the warm fragrance of *Rosa rugosa* fills my senses. My soul sets down to rest. I am at peace.

All the earth reflects His glory. If I can stop, rest and listen, I will watch it unfold each day before me, bringing healing and restoration. But I must give it more than a glance. I must give Him the chance to dwell within me, allow Him to heal and restore me.

Nantucket touches His Spirit within you. This island is a piece, a small reflection of our final home where He dwells, the place for which my spirit longs. If only in part, having it here is a gift worth cherishing and carrying into my days ahead.

And like it or not, the very day the ferry returns me to its mainland slip, the ropes will be waiting for me, mooring me to my life in another home. If I have genuinely sought and learned of Him here, then I will take His renewed presence into the battles of life. I will take His purpose, go out again into His world to tell others about the Creator who has prepared a more beautiful, peaceful, and wondrous place than even this tiny sanctuary in the Atlantic.

Here in the beauty, His touch is so evident. I see Him at each bend in the path. And I know so much more of his character and what He has prepared for us.

"No eye has seen, no ear has heard, no mind had conceived what God has prepared for those who love Him."

1 CORINTHIANS 2:9

Chapter Two

Great Point

"Unless the Lord builds the house, its builders labor in vain."

PSALM 127:1

I have memories of being a child on this island. The Great Point light stands proudly behind me, guarding its treacherous waters. The warm, soft sand, silhouetted by beach grass and colorful banks of poison ivy, marks the path to the beach where dunes stand like mountains between the lighthouse and the water.

I remember running and tumbling down the dunes to the beach below. Legs flying, my footprints abruptly vanishing from the crest, I'd launch myself into the air and land proudly in the warm sand, sometimes buried clear up to my knees. Then I'd run down the rest of the dune so fast I couldn't stop before reaching the water's edge. Diving into the cold sea, I'd come up gasping from the chill. Then I'd dash off for the top of the dune again, thrilled just to repeat the game once more.

The water wasn't always cold, but it was always crystal clear. I could find the best stones on the island by lazily floating at the water's edge, letting the waves come and go, pulling up handful upon handful of glistening treasures from the bottom. When the sea was calm, I could stand chest-deep and see my toes staring proudly back up at me amid the mosaic of stones and sand.

I don't remember the long drive to the island. And my memories of the ferry are mostly of sleeping and being awakened to see who could be first to spot the Great Point Light. But what I do remember was the long, bumpy, and crowded Jeep ride to the Point.

Our first night was often spent in the Sconset house if we didn't take the morning boat. The upper levels were filled with wooden cubbies where we slept like nesting rabbits. A rambling old structure, the living room sported a canopy of latticework on the ceiling. Eye-level to me was a big stone fireplace, usually with a fire burning. Across the room, cushioned window seats overlooked the stubby lawn that challenged even the most skilled croquet player. The kitchen was a small galley, but the food was always plentiful, and the laughter of sun-tanned faces filled the big dining room table. These were my parents' special friends, Gene and Eleanor, the ones who first brought us to this sandy outpost.

The following day, we'd stuff ourselves into their old Willys Jeep. Groceries, dog, adults, and children alike would set out for the "Shack," our friends' home in the dunes of Great Point. These Jeep rides were often one of my few opportunities to hear adult conversation, since this time, privacy had indeed escaped my parents' grasp. Their talk usually started with the latest weather report, moved onto the past year's events, and then centered on us kids. Ultimately, however, it always led to the status of the Galls and the tide. I never quite understood what the Galls were and why the tide mattered if we were on land, but the adults always became very serious when they spoke about the Galls.

In those days, you had to make passage to Great Point at low tide. Only then was the narrow spit of sand, the Galls, that connected the main island to Great Point clear of the water. Later in life, the Galls became filled with permanent sand, so we didn't have to discuss it in the Jeep anymore. But to this day, when I pass this place on our way to Great Point, I remember those discussions on our early morning rides to the Shack.

The Shack was Gene's creation. Built mostly out of driftwood that had washed ashore, it stood anchored to the dune by a hand-built stone fireplace, much like the one in the Sconset house. I wasn't around when the Shack was being constructed, so I don't know how long it took. And I don't ever remember anyone believing me when I said that Gene had built it himself. But those of us who met him knew that it was true. And it didn't matter because we believed it.

Inside was close quarters. There was only one room, and the fireplace took up most of it. The stones were much bigger than the cup of my two hands, rounded and worn by the waves. The mortar, I assumed, was beach sand. Somewhere off the living room was the galley. And though I never was quite clear where, I did see Gene and Eleanor disappear and reappear with food and beverage from behind the fireplace. The living room also served as the bedroom, which was good, since I usually fell asleep after dinner, exhausted from the fresh air, swimming, and climbing the dunes.

Gene had dug a well, but of course, there was no electricity, so we got used to the soft glow of kerosene lamps and the odd smell they made. The adults also were very serious about these lamps. I wasn't worried. I knew that Gene had a powerful light that ran on a mighty battery if he needed to go out in the rain at night.

Gene and Eleanor must have been great friends with my parents when I think of all of us in that house. They also had a large black poodle, Windy, who would bump us over when he got on a tear. I was always a little intimidated by Windy, probably because he was bigger than I for so many of those years. And also because I knew that if Gene wasn't watching, and Windy decided that he wanted the sandwich in my hand, it was his.

In the evenings, we'd sing songs in front of the fire in the

Shack. My favorite was the one Gene and my dad made up from the tune "My Father was the Keeper of the Eddystone Light." We sang it to the Great Point Light. Later, when we took car trips as a family, we'd sing that song and the others we'd learned in the firelight of those evenings. I was long into my adult years before I realized that the song wasn't written about the Great Point Light.

At night, we slept in separate guest quarters called "Double Trouble." Like the Shack, the beds were lowered down off the walls and held by chains. I thought this was terribly exciting. Although climbing into those upper bunks was not easy. Double Trouble was also just one room. It sat closer to the inlet, away from the lighthouse, and down from the Shack. I remember being able to ride the waves in the inlet on a windy day and not being afraid. The water was warm like our baths at home, shallow and safe.

Gene was what my parents called an engineer. As a child, I knew that my grandfather was an engineer. We would go to the train station on Saturdays and watch him pull in the special trains he ran from New York to Philadelphia. Craning our necks, we'd wait for his happy face to peak out of the small window as he pulled the magnificent engine to a stop. He would wave at us from atop the diesel, and we felt so proud.

Somehow, I knew that Gene was an engineer because he also was spoken of with great reverence by everyone. He was the keeper of the Shack. He dug the well and ran the pump for the water. And he even kept the fire burning and the stove working. He and his great light guided us on foggy nights back to Double Trouble. I never knew how he did all these things; they just seemed to be done mysteriously, kind of like when he'd get us across the Galls. All of this was enough to bring reverence to my eyes.

As an adult, I know a little about what technical engineers can do. But I am still in awe of the man who created a home out of driftwood far off in the dunes and who was generous enough to share it with all of us. How like our Father in heaven was this man. Big and strong and knowledgeable about all mysteries. Provider of water, heat, food, and protection. Keeper of the light for us. Warm and generous with his life.

In those days, one of our paths to the beach ran right past the lighthouse. If I was nimble and minded the poison ivy, I could walk right up to the base of the Great Point light, take my hand and smack it against the solid stone. And sometimes, if I were lucky and timed it just right, I would even get to go up to the top with the lighthouse keeper. But, because in those days, the existence of the light was never in question, we didn't pay it much attention except at night, when like moths, we would try to follow the light around its circular path.

The dunes were long and wide and high then. Two dunes separated the Shack from the sea. No one would have believed it if you'd said that in the years to come, the Shack would be gone. But as time went on, the wind and the seas tore at those dunes, and one day the Shack went back into the sea.

For a long time, only the stone fireplace remained. Around it, we'd built our lives, the light of friendship, the warmth of love, and the hand of the Lord that provided. It tore at my heart to see it standing there alone, without us, as if someone had torn off the pages of our memories and exposed them to the wind and rain. Ultimately, even the stones and wood found their place once more in the sea.

Yet even though the Shack has returned to the ocean, its labor was not in vain. For a house that the Lord builds stands forever, even if only in the memories of the days and nights that were warmed by the people I loved.

"For every house is built by someone, but
God is the builder of everything."

HEBREWS 3:4

Chapter Three

Stones

"Where were you when I laid the earth's foundation? . . . Who shut up the sea behind doors when it burst forth from the womb, . . . when I said, 'This far you may come and not farther; here is where your proud waves halt'?"

JOB 38:4,8,11

The artistry of the Lord is irresistible to my senses. Each day's tide paints a landscape of scattered stones whose randomness and balance even the best artist cannot imitate. Walking the beach, my eyes frequently are drawn to sets of stones—a large one juxtaposed in perfect harmony with a smaller one or a group of small stones nestled close to a larger one.

Around and under some of the stronger ones, the waves carve eddies, making it appear as if they have a place of permanence superior to their more minor sisters and brothers. My heart is drawn to the large stones in compassion. I remember those "large people" in my life who thought their weight in power and financial status insulated them from the tides of life. But as with those stones, a final wave carried them off to a place of humility and acquiescence. God's power is the only one that cannot be broken. Ours never withstands the test.

Each of my stones has been washed smooth by thousands of rubbings against others in the sea. Some, cast up by the last wave, sit poised at the outermost edge of the tide's reach, elevated on a fragile rim of sand, now dried by the sun. As I stoop to touch this miniature berm, even the soft caress of my finger collapses the tiny crust of sand, and the delicate boundary is once more lost into the beach.

Sometimes I hear myself speculating about where each stone originated. How like the stars in the sky they are, lying about in constellations, waiting for my eye's attention. Often, I find a smaller picture painted within a constellation. A white or caramel stone will have a piece of green seaweed basking on its surface as if an artist had carefully laid it there when wet.

Such is the Master's thought to focus my attention on more minor things, lest I miss a vital lesson of discovery.

Leaving the cool, wet sand, I strike out for the upper beach. Here the stones are dry and warm. Much like the surrounding sand, these stones do not call out for close inspection. They are dull and muted, unlike those on the tidal edge that glisten with each fresh wave. These are the everyday stones. Only a storm will wash them back onto the lower beach, where they will be shaped and polished, displaying their full beauty.

How like my life are these stones. At certain times, I have felt discarded and dull, of use to no one, including God. I needed a storm to move me into God's purpose. Then pounded by waves and a roaring sea, when I next wash up, I glisten with radiant beauty, the polish of Living Water.

Sometimes my stint on the lower beach lasts a long time. But only when I am fully spent will I be thrown onto the upper beach to rest awhile. How fickle I am! First, I yearn to change and grow, and then I yearn only for the calm of the upper beach. How grateful I am for the Master who chooses the storms of life to complete His purposes and lets me rest between washings!

Each stone has been placed on the beach. But not every stone will be worn smooth, tossed and displaced, or left on the upper beach. He walks the beach every day looking at the stones, picking them up, and putting them into His hand. He's looking for His children. He wants to build His holy city.

"You also, like living stones, are being built into a spiritual house to be a holy priesthood,"

1 PETER 2:5

Chapter Four

Marsh House

"He leads me beside quiet waters, he restores my soul."

PSALM 23:2-3

A small marsh borders a dirt road not far from my daily journeys. At its edge, a gray shingled house sits looking out to the sea. I wonder about the happenings of this marsh, the wildlife that visits for sustenance, and the people who wake up to its beauty each day. I'm sure it has a cadre of secret admirers, though I suspect it is known mainly by those of us on foot.

While the marsh lies beyond my usual walk, I often choose this destination as its tranquil beauty soothes my weariness. The water in the marsh varies in expanse depending upon the spring and summer rains. But regardless of its size, the small pond is always framed with an abundance of pink swamp mallows and tall cattails bronzed by the sun.

Inner access to the marsh is by a soggy deer trail from the dirt road, inviting only the curious. Diving through the dense scrub, the heady fragrance of sweet pepper bush and swamp honeysuckle fills the air around me. In the fall, the pungent scent of wild grapes will suddenly turn my head to seek its source. Deep in the recesses of the marsh, the reeds are thick, and the chatter of yellowthroat warblers and rufous breasted towhees escapes from the scrub oak around its edges.

Gazing across the marsh, my eye is filled with a multitude of velvet grasses, their texture punctuated only by the green leaves and deep pink of the swamp mallows and the sky dipping blue into the still water. In the fall, the greens melt into russet and gold. Most of the mallows have bloomed, though one can usually find a few flowers sheltered in the warm recesses of the marsh.

Soon large green buds with black seeds will stand in their place, waiting for next year's blossoms. Already, tiny seedlings grow rakishly along the path. I wonder if the deer think about what they are treading on as they slip through here for a drink. And I wonder what feeds this marsh, what source of living water supplies freshness and life to all the creatures around.

I think I should like living by the marsh. It is small and containable, unlike the others on the island, shared by so many footprints. I could gaze out over its stillness to the sand and sea, my soul drinking in its beauty. I think I'd listen especially for the soft parting of the water as the mallards slip their feet below the surface so they can sun themselves in this quiet retreat and for the high-pitched song of the bumblebees in the mallows.

On many occasions, I've watched the bees helicopter in and out of those pink petals, hovering over each flower as if contemplating its bounty. Once ensconced in that heavenly crown of pollen, they scrabble around with absolute revelry. At first, I suspected the bees had some unique way of tracking which flowers they'd visited. For often, when finished with a particular flower, instead of choosing to stop at the nearest neighbor, they'd select another flower, seemingly at random. But then, one day watching one enter a flower, I heard it let out a high-pitched whine and fly off as if annoyed with itself for forgetting it had stopped there before. Maybe unbeknownst to us, the flowers free of nectar give off a different scent that only close inspection reveals to the bees. Or perhaps it's their way of openly commenting upon their friends who have already flown off with the golden nectar.

It makes me wonder about their sharing, and whether like hummingbirds, bees mark out certain flower territories as their own. Whatever the case, they are a class unto themselves. And unlike the yellow jackets, which just seem so fiercely territorial in their attack of the wild grapes, the bumblebees seem to appreciate the beauty of the mallows.

On the island, I find that I am like the bumblebees, delighting in the blessings and wonder around me, thanking God for the provision He has made for me. Yet off-island, I can become like the yellow jackets, fierce, focused, and not always appreciative of the people and world around me. I fly so fast that I miss the beauty, not only of the flowers but also of the people in my path. I'm so intent on my own mission that I miss His journey.

Beside the still water in the pool of Bethsaida, Jesus asked the crippled man if he wanted to be healed. His response evaded the question and begged an excuse. I wonder how often I have avoided being healed of the world and its influence on my life by that same water because I did not honestly believe I could live separate from the world.

Jesus knew His mission. He had confidence in the Father that together they would accomplish it. But He never missed a moment on the journey. I am grateful for these days when I can walk with Him along the dirt roads, walk the beaches and slow down. They create a longing in me to practice a life different from the "Autobahn" in which I live on the mainland. These daily journeys provide a pool of solace and a grateful peace that I can draw upon for healing when He faces me with the questions, "Do you want to be healed of this worldly life? Do you want to abide in Me even though I cannot take you out of this world?" By the marsh, I hear Jesus saying, "Be still, cease striving, and know that I am God." Perhaps I shouldn't complain when I can't hear Him or when I don't know His will. He *is* God. But I am *rarely* still.

From the beach, the marsh is hidden from sight. Only a subtle change in the dune and the sweet knowledge of its presence can lure me from the water's edge. The marsh reaches toward the beach in a dry wash, surrounded by a small dune blanketed with beach grass. Close to the freshwater, the sand and mud are mixed. But out by the dune, the sand is dry and full of the ocean's skeletons left on the upper beach.

As I enter the wash, I'm walking in a warm canyon carved out of the sand. Sitting down to rest, I begin to imprint on my memory the view of the mallows, the house, and the sky reflected in the still water. The dune hides the pounding of the ocean. It is quiet.

Today, a brown mallard lifts his wings and shoots his long neck forward as if anticipating I will disturb the solitude he has found with his mate. I also enjoy the late afternoon sun on the marsh and am quiet, so I don't scare them. In October, the ducks and I will have the place to ourselves. Even the dragonflies will have turned in their wings.

Heading back to the beach, the sheltered warmth from the dunes radiates from my feet and envelops my figure. The beach grass cresting the dune billows with the wind off the ocean. I cannot even feel it, so sheltered am I from the beach. The grasses are silver-green, the tip of each blade dipped in sunlight. Some, slightly bent, are leaving patterns in the sand reminiscent of our childhood attempts at making angel wings in the snow, both reminding the passersby of their certain places in existence.

How universal is the wind in the grass. I watch it across the pond from my desk in the house. I remember it on the hillside across the bay in Antigua, looking like the mane of a lion billowing in the breeze. Or better yet, an army of small creatures runs underneath the grass, rolling it like a wave.

In September, these grasses will be heavy with seed and ripe for harvest, each at His command. For a brief moment, I stood gazing at this sunlit harvest, framed by the strip of soft sand, a sea of lapis lazuli, the sky a faded robin's egg blue. Not a cloud was caught in the expanse.

The richness of that beauty, the healing of its presence, is well beyond human words. It carries His supernatural being and dwells in our spirit like nothing of our own making can ever quite do. I have always felt His invisible presence when walking amidst such beauty, even before His Spirit came to dwell within me. Looking back, I think it was my umbilical cord to Him. Seeing the world through His eyes kept me until the day when I would be cleansed and restored to full sight.

I am reluctant to leave the marsh and return home, even to my cozy house. For, in some way, it means a return to ordinary reality. In my visit, I have filled my being with His stillness, the very presence of His purpose. I have stored it up for those days off island when I become just a little too busy, too restless, or too much distressed with the world in which I must live. Jesus said, "My prayer is not that you take them out of the world, but that you protect them from the evil one. For they are not of the world, even as I am not of it." (John 17:15-16)

In some senses, the world of the marsh is a piece of His protection. While I cannot physically live in its presence, I can carry it within me as I live back on the mainland. Then I can offer it up to the world as a gift. For that prayer and that gift, I am grateful.

> *"Whoever drinks the water I give him, will never thirst. Indeed, the water I give him will become in him a spring of water welling up to eternal life."*
>
> JOHN 4:14

Chapter Five

Pink Sea Crab

"Are not two sparrows sold for a penny? Yet not one of them will fall to the ground apart from the will of your Father."

MATTHEW 10:29

The ebb of high tide brings an array of sea presents scattered along the wet sand. Silent among the smooth glistening stones, I find a small, rose-spotted crab on its back. Speculating on its life, I flip it over. It gratefully regains its firm position among the sand particles.

While it was hard for me to leave it alone on its back, I paused momentarily before touching its life. In those few moments, I caught myself wondering if somehow I would be tampering with the natural order of things to rescue it from the rising sun. Was it lying in my path as its specific destiny for that day? Did I interrupt some personal plan of extinction that was unknown to me?

Speculating about this, I remembered that at creation, the natural order was governed by life. Through man's disobedience, death entered into creation, temporarily removing the eternal life that began in the Garden. God's order was corrupted, and a new natural order, survival of the fittest, was initiated.

While He desires to give us eternal life, the present order of things ultimately brings death to us all. We know that all creation groans for His return, and we, too, long for that new heaven and earth. For me, even the tiny rescue of a pink sea crab stands as a victory against the present nature of things, an indication of the life to come.

I rescued the crab. Washed up, abandoned, vulnerable. How many times have I been picked up, put aright, and given another chance by His hands? I think of Jesus by the Sea of Galilee. How many lost and abandoned did He put right? To how many people left "high and dry" by the tides of life would He give new life? More than the grains of the sand in the sea.

Later, after miles of beach, I once more happen upon the

same pink crab clinging to the wet sand. Picking up its body, careful to stay clear of its defensive pinchers, I toss it seaward. God's hand or mine? No question this time.

I suspect my response to this crab is a small reflection of my own desire for self-importance. While I may become quite adept at acknowledging God's sovereignty, I frequently slip into thinking that I can somehow alter His plan for the universe, even through such a small event as the life of a tiny crab. I forget about His caring for the sparrow. I forget about His omniscience and compassion. Instead, I place my own sense of importance on the events of the day, thus magnifying my significance. I pretend to occupy a place in eternity that is not mine.

Was it not He who created the beach, placed the crab in the cold waters, and sent me to Nantucket to walk the beach? Absolutely. His ever-present knowledge of my appearance on the beach that morning, that I would send the little pink crab sailing through the sky back into its cold water to crawl the ocean floor again is the miracle of it all. Perhaps one day, that little crab will be washed ashore again. But perhaps not. That is not for me to say, a responsibility for which I am eternally grateful.

What a wondrous, mighty, and deeply compassionate God we have who would take the time to spend every moment with us throughout eternity. How foolish we are, and what wonders we miss by not acknowledging His very presence in all of our walks through life.

Do you imagine that Jesus and the disciples always talked about important things on those long, dusty walks between hillsides? No, they spoke of little things that came their way, the sparrow singing in a thorn bush, the baby lamb nuzzling its mother, or even the wildflowers blooming in the fields. All creation is His. He is in all things. And He, in His limitless generosity, wants to share them with us. Well then, let's allow Him to be sovereign over the big and the small.

I do not suppose that the life and death of a pink sea crab are of any less importance to Him or any less deserving of His attention than the carving of the Grand Canyon or the snow on Mount Everest. And I am grateful for that. For in the scheme of things, I think my life is much more like that of the pink sea crab.

"But God chose the foolish things of the world to shame the wise; God chose the weak things of the world to shame the strong."

1 CORINTHIANS 1:27

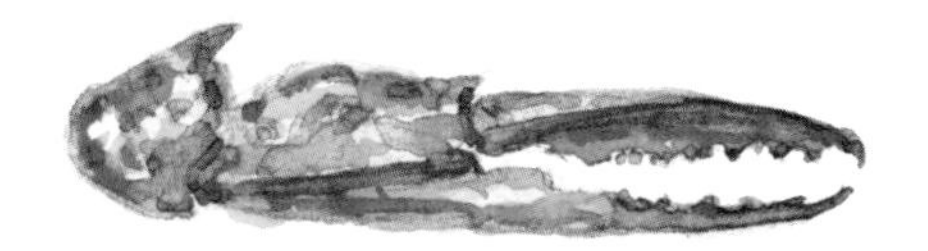

Chapter Six

The Extraordinary

"Now to him who is able to do immeasurably more than all we ask or imagine,"

EPHESIANS 3:20

How tiresome it is to listen to people who expect the worst! Every day, ominous reports ranging from the weather to economics or politics assault our psyche. What a burden it creates for our souls to carry! Our spirit must fight extra battles not to listen and become of the same mind.

Just try to convince someone that a northeaster may not hit. That the snow won't be as deep as the weatherman says. That life is not tough and stressful, and that we should be so glad that God gave us this day. Just try it. You'll see what I mean.

I am amazed at how much energy we devote to this pessimistic outlook. And as a result, how much of life do we miss? We cloak ourselves with it every day, from the point of stepping out of the shower to closing our eyes at night. Why?

God has given us a marvelous creation. Look at your children playing in the ocean. Take up a moon shell and explain why its spiral winds in a perfect destiny to some infinite center point. Explain why a hermit crab chooses to live in one shell rather than another and how it gets washed up on the beach from miles away. Lie down on the grass on an August night and watch the cavalcade of shooting stars move across the deep sky. It's pretty hard to be negative and blasé for long.

I'm convinced that no one will disagree or complain in heaven. There won't be anything in another person that we don't like. Contentment will reign. After all, the Father and the Son and the Spirit always agree. So why can't we?

In addition, heaven will be so beautiful that we won't need words. So there will be lovely hours of silence when no one is trying to sell you something or complain about something, or distract you from enjoying your day.

This is what I was musing about one day as I headed out

from the house up the dirt road. Approaching the mammoth puddle that guards my cottage, I noted how the splashes had coated the leaves of the nearby vines and scrub. As I deftly walked around the thin grass perimeter of the puddle, I took a closer look at the scrub. And I saw for the first time something so extraordinary that I stood with my mouth open. There in front of me, mud-splattered but still brilliant, was the porcelain berry vine.

Its beauty is so striking that I really could not quite believe my eyes. Nowhere in nature do you find berries of robin's egg blue, deep purple, rosy pink, and porcelain white, all clustered together and embedded in a wreath of deep green leaves. Perfectly rounded, speckled with deeper hues, the berries cover the scrub, overflowing its branches, decorating the brush with their pearls of color.

How coincidental, I thought. Just when I was getting so tired of people complaining and expecting the very worst of life, instead of the best, God sends the most extraordinary beauty one could find on a summer's day. As if to say, "Yes, this life is a gift, and if you look amidst all the mud, there am I. Extraordinary. Beautiful. Bountiful and waiting for your discovery. Don't spend time expecting the worst, talking about how bad things are, complaining. Look, praise, and be glad. It's what I intended for you all along."

"Sing to the Lord a new song, for he has done marvelous things;"

PSALM 98:1

Chapter Seven

Pond Edge

"Be strong and courageous. Do not be terrified; do not be discouraged, for the Lord your God will be with you wherever you go."

JOSHUA 1:9

I walked the edge of the pond today. Contemplating this journey, I've been studying its sandy rim for several days, building up anticipation about whether I could walk its perimeter or if it would become an impenetrable marsh and bar my passage. The goal was to journey at least three-quarters of the way around and provide an easy walk for Gillie, my aging but zealous poodle.

In some respects, the edge of a pond is quite ordinary, its shoreline more stable than the ever-changing beachfront. Often a history of days or weeks is still evident, presenting a kaleidoscope of stories about the season past. Edges of stones, sticks and general flotsam tell of multiple storms and high-water marks.

Unlike the ocean, which rakes its creatures and plants from the deep, a pond's shoreline is much subtler in its story. And sometimes, such ordinary treasures lend themselves more easily to God's teaching since I am not so intent on gaining a new visual discovery from my surroundings. The sheer disappointment of comparing my speculation and fantasy with reality often gives me a sharper spiritual adventure than when the impression of physical beauty moves me.

In point of fact, the walk was a gift of solitude and isolation. And on this occasion, I did make it three-quarters of the way around. But at the farthest point, I encountered one of isolation's favorite companions, fear. Staring up at me, leading out of the scrub and disappearing down the beach were the footprints of a *very, very,* large dog. Fresh footprints. And no human tracks accompanying it. Pausing briefly on this thought, I remembered that our adversary, the devil, often leaves tracks to spawn fear and distract us from spiritual gifts that the Father intends for us. Capturing these thoughts in prayer, Gillie and I pressed onward.

The real prize of the day was the close-up view of the osprey's nest. Standing below the nest, I gazed up at the messy jumble of sticks, thinking how untidy it looked compared with the view I'd had of it from the deck using my field glasses! I suppose I should have been prepared for its size since it stood out even to the naked eye from a mile away. But I wasn't. With their lofty view of sea, sky, and pond, sticks all akimbo, those lucky nestlings sit on top of the world. I was charmed.

While there appeared to be no renter for the nest, I still found myself wondering. What is it like to lie in that nest, waiting for the lighthouse beam to display the water in the pond and ocean, resting briefly on the housetops and Sankaty Golf Club, and then carefully repeating its journey? Do the nestlings welcome its friendship or long for deep fog so they can sleep undisturbed? Certainly, I am drawn into my own living room to watch that beam of light if I wake in the night. And I am uneasy if the light barely penetrates the night when the fog lies heavily over the pond.

For a good part of the walk beyond the osprey's nest, a set of deer tracks provided evidence of a companion along the rim of the pond. It appeared that an enormous buck had been walking the water's edge late last night. Its cloven prints were a good two inches long and an inch and a half deep. How majestic it must have been, framed in the moonlight by the pond!

Ultimately the edge of the pond did reach into the marshes, and I was forced to abandon my hope of circumnavigating it to those with hip boots and little fear of snapping turtles.

But I was satisfied and even beginning to wonder if our feet and paws would last the long walk home.

When I finally reached the ocean beach, I was weary from the long hike in the sand. Thinking I could shorten my path by crossing the inlet that was left when the pond was opened to the sea, I contemplated the possibility of jumping from my slim spit of sand to the other side. But the channel was deeper than usual, and I dared not risk throwing both Gillie and myself into the drink just to save a few steps.

The white herons that earlier were stalking lunch in the shallows had disappeared with the sun. The gulls were beginning to gather on the shore for the night. My speculation over, my gifts received, Gillie and I walked home slowly, remembering the day's adventure, knowing exactly what lies on the other side of the pond.

"We demolish arguments and every pretension that sets itself up against the knowledge of God, and we take captive every thought to make it obedient to Christ."

2 CORINTHIANS 10:5

Chapter Eight

Champ

"Follow me!"

JOHN 21:19

At the end of the dirt road, where its passage turns away from the beach, a large standing field is marked off by a weathered and broken fence. It is a long walk to reach this part of the beach road, but I come here in autumn to drink in the sea of goldenrod and watch the goldfinches raid the milkweed pods. I am drawn to this field because it reminds me of my childhood days with Champ, a large pinto horse that came to live with us one year.

Standing in the tall grass, my arms abreast of the rough grey rails, I think of those days, golden like the field that spreads out before me. During those days, the flowering grasses would often fool me into thinking that an insect had invited itself to dance upon my knees. When the tickling of its tiny feet and wings got my attention, I would take a quick swat at my knees or stamp my legs like the horses. Today, still like that child, I catch myself doing this several times before I realize that the grass has tricked me once again.

Usually, about this time in my reverie, a big pinto horse hearing my stamping would raise his head from the sweet grass and crane his long neck around toward his rump, staring straight at me, ears alert for my whistle. Then without a second's pause, he would turn and lazily lope toward me, muscles rippling, his white and chestnut spots running into each other as if someone had just poured chocolate syrup onto ice cream. I named him Champ, and well it suited him, for he was the image of my own personal champion, the one I had ridden on journeys as a child.

Coming closer to me, I stroke his velvet nose, punctuated by a few white whiskers, observe those straight white eyelashes, and wonder what mysteries hide behind his brown marble eyes.

Sometimes I'd lay my face alongside his muscular neck and hug him, shoulder to shoulder, smelling the warm hay and sweat in his coat. So enveloped, I felt safe, loved, and protected. I never could figure out how he tolerated the flies on his face and eyes, so I'd swish them away to give him relief. I guess in some ways, all of us are plagued with flies. I wonder how many flies the Master brushed off my face that I didn't acknowledge or even know about.

There's something comforting about an animal that responds to your presence by coming happily over to you as you stand by the fence. As a child, I remember my horse, Champ, being taller than I, more solid, more secure with himself, and always glad to see me. I felt safe on his back and knew he wouldn't betray me. I was confident of the journeys that we took together in his field. He showed me all of what he saw each day. I think that if asked, he'd say that his boundaries were drawn in pleasant places. And I was grateful to have him as my guide to his world.

A fence is a perfect jumping-off spot for a child. Two steps and a quick leap, and I could be astride Champ. I remember the first time riding bareback, being so stunned at his girth, but not nearly so shocked as when I slid off at the end of our ride and suddenly remembered all the witty remarks I'd made about TV cowboys. A little humility when dealing with the Champion is always best.

Once mounted on Champ's back, the trick was to get him into a lope instead of a trot. Of course, this was less work for me and more work for him, so we compromised often. Sometimes I'd pull forward onto his neck and hold onto his mane and pretend I was a jockey and we were racing the wind.

Occasionally something would startle him, or I'd forget where I was, and I would suddenly find myself in the weeds again, having slipped off, usually just shy of one of his previous day's leftovers. I suppose I felt like a fly to him since each time this happened, he'd just pull grass until I got up again. Usually, by then, we were far from the fence, so remounting was tougher.

My childhood Champ was the product of many months of persistently begging my parents. Later in life, when I also suffered from severe allergies, I was reminded of my father's sacrifice to have a horse and all the attendant hay and straw in the loft. My heart has a special place for the memory and sacrifices he made out of love. I am reminded of how faithful our Father in heaven is to provide the deepest desires of our hearts. And of the great sacrifice He made so we could have access to Him for such desires.

Champ brought responsibility into my life. I remember carting steaming manure in a wheelbarrow out of the barn, down below the pond's dam in two feet of snow. I remember currying Champ till his coat glistened, only to have him roll in the mud in the field. It's kind of like me with the Master.

We all learned something new from Champ. My mom, an expert at rising to the occasion, became the master of inserting Champ's bit. Somehow I think those big yellow teeth didn't intimidate her as much as me. And we all learned trust. I'm sure when my parents found out how far away I rode that it bothered them. But they always let me go.

God is our Champion. And while sometimes we don't always get what we ask for, the receipt of any gift brings His presence into our lives and the entrusted responsibility of using that gift wisely. I would never diminish the personal and financial sacrifice my parents made. It reflects the kind of love and eternal sacrifice God made in offering His son to die for me.

Standing in this field, I remember the warmth, love, and safety that my friend Champ provided and realize how much the Lord was there with me in so many ways, teaching me about Himself even before I came to know Him. For me, Champ still lives in this field, warmed by the sun, freshened by the sea breezes, and filled with green grass and wildflowers for food.

The field of goldenrod is empty today. But only to the casual observer. The Champion is always there, waiting to take me on yet another journey in His world.

"Lord, you have assigned me my portion and my cup; you have made my lot secure. The boundary lines have fallen for me in pleasant places; surely I have a delightful inheritance."

PSALM 16:5-6

Chapter Nine

Gates

*"I am the gate; whoever enters through me will be saved.
He will come in and go out, and find pasture."*

JOHN 10:9

Departing to the left and right, rising over hills into the sky, Nantucket's country driveways tug at my child-like curiosity to explore their grassy paths. The island is full of these entrances, enticing you like unopened letters, beckoning you to read on. Many of the entries are guarded by gates of varying style and character, much I suppose, a reflection of their owners' determination to keep away unwelcome visitors.

To me, the entrances that cut steady swaths of crushed white stone or imported bluestone appear aloof and forbidding, perhaps implying that I would be unwelcome in such rich habitations. Other drives open with the familiarity of the island's crushed scallop shells or a different sandy mixture of stones to keep the erosion in check. And still others, perhaps my favorites, carry on throughout the years as simple grassy tracks, filled here and there with puddles of worn stones to keep the ruts at bay. Two sand strips and a shorn border that hold back the encroaching grapevines and wild roses, these drives rise and curve into the scrub, leading my eye straight to cottages nestled snugly in the pines or dunes.

Gillie loves these entrances. Often stopping to sniff, she explores the grass while I pause to gather any fragrances in the air. Each opening tells a story to me. Usually, I try to imagine what the people who live there are like, making up stories of my own. Sometimes the mailbox reveals a clue, especially if it has been there for many years. The older homes often have only a stake with the owner's name painted on by hand.

Frequently, I can tell the early settlers by their lack of care over the sign or mailbox at the entrance, something that still reminds me of the more casual, generic days of the island 50 years ago. Other openings have large stones, the more recent ones carved with a name or number, the older ones often with only an iron ring that attaches to the gate to keep the winter winds from swinging it open and shut. And some entrances are free of gates, their owners apparently not concerned about intruders. Those I always imagine are guarded closer to home by a large golden retriever. Like warm memories, I return to these entrances over and over again, as if greeting old friends.

Many of the dirt roads I've walked hundreds of times. Each one has a favorite gate or entrance. Sometimes a small tidy gate conceals a deep path or tunnel through the scrub that leads from the mailbox back up to the house. Others sport trellises of roses or September's white clematis. Those that have gone wild sometimes have a blanket of grapevines and porcelain berry intermingled and rampant. The wide gates are usually split rail and weathered. Like the scrub oak, they show a mottled pattern of greens, grays, and yellows, where the lichens have danced on the wood to their hearts' content. The newer two-by-four gates, painted red, will only need a year or so of neglect before they too begin to look more like their surroundings.

It is not that I do not enjoy the cared-for beauty that the newer homes bring to the island. But like the downtown area, I find its worldliness a stark contrast with the more natural beauty the island uniquely possesses. And some of these gates, located in the open valleys and meadows of Madequecham, cling to my memory because of the broad glorious vistas they display and the sense of freedom I feel when standing at their entrances. Each time I encounter these favorite entryways, they draw me forward to explore the beauty contained within them and perhaps hear the story of the people who live just beyond the gate.

Life inside these gates is one of family and history. Each has a story to tell of how they came to love this island and what refreshment it provides them. Outside our gates, we are vulnerable and alone in a world that is unfamiliar with our authentic selves. These gates mark off passages to sanctuaries we have found or built away from the outside world. World-weary travelers like myself enter these sanctuaries longing to find rest.

In the gospel of John, Jesus speaks of the sheepfold. Only the good shepherd can freely go in and out of the gate. The watchman at the gate responds only to the Shepherd's voice. The thief or robber must enter by some other way. The sheep know His voice and follow Him. They know that their life is safe and protected with Him. Like a sheep outside of Him, I am vulnerable to poachers and predators in my personal life and family. I spend so much of my life in that outer world. It is no wonder that I am drawn to create a sanctuary for my rest and restoration.

When Jesus died on the cross, the veil into the inner sanctuary was torn in two, allowing us to go in and find rest through Him. It is His desire that I find rest in Him. Each day I am faced with choices, entrances that lead me on either the narrow path toward Him or entice me on the broader path to self-sufficiency and materialism. Through the years, I have found that the latter brings physical or emotional exhaustion, and ultimately, some form of personal destruction. Each day I have a choice to go in and out of His sheepfold, to find pasture, or to think I can find it on my own. It cannot be found in the outside world. It is a false hope pervaded by thieves and robbers in the world's clothing.

When I was a child, my father and I would take long hikes together in the woods and mountains. Usually, well into the walk and the day, one of us would tire and ask if we should start back. The other would reluctantly agree but suggest that we go just around the corner or to the top of the next hill for the view and then turn around. There just might be something special waiting around the corner. Once we arrived at our agreed-upon destination, the one who'd proposed going home would sheepishly suggest that we hike around yet one more corner. And so it would go, and we would be another mile down the trail until we both admitted that the sun was setting and we would have to finish the hike another day.

Such curiosity for the next turn was bred in those hikes. Neither of us wanted to miss anything unique that might be hiding around the corner. That same curiosity caused my parents and me to linger long hours in the moors looking for birds and wildflowers. Today, without them here, a distraction such as the sound of a yellowthroat singing in the scrub may cause me to temporarily pause and consider the length of my journey. But often, the tantalizing thought of a view of the ocean from a high knoll spurs me on just a little farther. Or sometimes it is simply that Gillie has high-tailed it down the grassy track in search of the most recent rabbit, and I must retrieve her.

Today, an old wooden gate stands before me. Thrown open against the scrub, it announces the owner's presence and draws me in for a closer look. The wood is still firm but silvered and rutted by the salt and wind. The rusted metal latches are worn with use but still functional. My small excursion to look and feel the wood of the gate reveals a family of towhees chirping instructions and responses to one another amidst the scrub oak. Two parents and two fledglings are quickly darting and dropping from branch to branch, calling to one another amid a flutter of wings. The rich color of the parents starkly contrasts with the mottled silver of the oak branches. The deep, black pitch on the father sets off the warmth of the female's chestnut feathers, lending a depth of coloring not often found on an island known chiefly for its fog and sand.

Discovering my presence, the towhees fly elsewhere. I am left musing once again about where this track in the scrub oak will lead. Like a child, my curiosity pulls me to the top of the hill. Below there is more track, a house, and the ocean. Somewhere I hear that bright "chewink" of the towhees again, and I head back to the dirt road, mindful that like the birds, most of us have sought the privacy of the scrub to enjoy our families and home without visitors.

Of all the personages and gates, only one leads to heaven. As tempting as some entrances into secret gardens may be, as plush as the lifestyle may appear, or as familiar as the grassy tracks may seem, only one path needs to be found. I am grateful that He who created the towhees and the scrub oak also placed in me a longing for that path and an ability to hear and recognize His voice. Knowing the Shepherd's voice when it beckons me, opens the gate and allows me to enter. There I will find His joy and rest.

"Enter through the narrow gate. For wide is the gate and broad is the road that leads to destruction, and many enter through it. But small is the gate and narrow the road that leads to life, and only a few find it."

MATTHEW 7:13-14

Chapter Ten

Northeaster

"The seas have lifted up, O Lord, the seas have lifted up their voice; the seas have lifted up their pounding waves. Mightier than the thunder of the great waters, mightier than the breakers of the sea—the Lord on high is mighty."

PSALM 93:3-4

Sitting in my living room, a warm coffee mug in hand, I am listening and watching as a northeaster buffets my tiny house. At this point, it is more sound and fury than rain. Everything that is a bit loose on the house rattles or gently bumps against its frame. The chimney has a soft hollow echo as the wind catches its open mouth and dives down its throat, searching for a peaceful home. The furnace's friendly hum coming on and off encourages me, and I am grateful for its faithful warmth.

From my cozy vantage point, I can watch how each shrub, grassy hillock, and hedgerow reacts to the wind. My favorite *Rosa rugosa* that cheers the borders of the deck has been stripped of its bright fuchsia wings. A few hapless petals still bend wearily at its side. Fully open to the rain, the yellow anthers that yesterday harvested a steady chatter of honeybees now salute the rain with golden tears, tiny pieces of pollen dotting the pink petals, and green leaves. My soul admires its staunch persistence to bloom amidst such rain and fog. Perhaps, unlike my own frail strength in the storms of life, it considers only one purpose—to bloom—and refuses to accept any other. Such perseverance has indeed produced great character, and even more, hope.

I find myself wondering whether the honeybees are curled up next to each other to keep warm in their hives. And are they hungry without being able to gather their pollen? Do they fast on these days? How do they occupy themselves? Maybe they talk of the sunshine to encourage each other. If God's faithfulness extends toward even the sparrows and admonishes us not to worry about food or clothing, He must have an excellent plan for the bees as well.

Nantucket is an island of groomed hedges and manicured lawns. But amidst a storm, such stately persistence leads to victory by the angry wind. All things must learn to bend with the Father's hand. The silhouette of the *Rosa rugosa* hedge about the deck looks a bit like a green Labrador retriever with his nose to the wind. His two front paws that sit on the open bench leap backward each time the wind sweeps his face. The Russian olive shimmers with each pass of the wind, its silver wings shaking like aspen leaves, its upper limbs flailing in the wind. Most of the top branches are bare, stripped of life by previous storms.

How like our lives are these plants. Quickly appearing storms race through our days, making us bend, often at the knees. Sometimes as we receive the gusts, our thorns scratch those around us. And indeed, sometimes our topmost priorities lose their splendor, and we recognize that we too need tighter pruning. Storm winds search out everything in our lives that is not securely fastened to the Vine, stripping off the dead works. His voice surrounds me today as I watch creation respond to the movement of His hand. How do I respond to such buffeting? Do I bend or stand? Do I yield to His will or die in my own?

Every once in a while, the mockingbird tries to sit on the phone wire by the garden shed. Precariously balanced, his tail bobbing up and down, he makes a determined effort to steady himself against the strong wind. I wonder why he chooses to come out in such a gale. Perhaps a temporary lull foolishly drew him out in search of food or song. And like most of us, when we have made a mistake that is displayed to the world, we mount up our proud feathers like the mockingbird and pretend that the wind is not blowing as hard as it is. And like the mockingbird, we are humbled by our own poor efforts to fight the wind and must ultimately retreat to safety.

When I step out before He prepares the path, it should come as no surprise that I am buffeted about in a storm. I do not determine the calling out, nor can I stand alone. It is one thing to be like Peter called out upon the waves into His waiting arms. It is quite another to strike out into a storm on my own, pretending that I am the Lone Ranger or that I am on some special errand.

Unfortunately, I think I am more like the mockingbird than Peter. Often I am so anxious to do something, anything, that I move too quickly. God promised Joshua that if he obeyed His commands, He would go before, behind, and beside him. What more can I ask? The key is obedience, especially when I am feeling a sense of urgency to act.

The rain has begun to pelt against the screens. One or two large drops have left a vertical path of miniature windowpanes where the water is caught in the screen openings. Quickly, the wind follows the drops' path, evaporating some of the tiny windowpanes as if someone had written a message in Braille. Then in an instant, it is gone. The wind has taken the Braille particles. The screen is left with a scramble of messages, but none so fine as the first message that appeared and disappeared like the trail of a falling star. How alert I must be to His voice and vision! Like the Hebrew runner, if I take my eyes off Him, I will miss the blessing. How many blessings have I missed because my face was turned away from the Father or because my eyes were not fixed on "Jesus, the author and perfecter of our faith"? (Hebrews 12:2)

Outside one of my windows, a shock of woodbine has grown up the house wall and skillfully poked itself between the storm sash and the windowpanes. Its bottom half, fully exposed, is whipped about by the storm, the leaves torn and weary. Oblivious to the carnage below, its top half is happily silhouetted in the light, undisturbed, its stillness a stark contrast to the frantic stem. Like the woodbine, we fool ourselves into thinking that we are safe, when in fact, we have left ourselves exposed. Jesus said, "I am the vine; you are the branches. If you remain in me and I in you, you will bear much fruit; apart from me you can do nothing." (John 15:5)

I fear we do not always choose to dwell in the Vine. Believing we are saved, we leave our souls exposed to the wiles of sin and the storms it will bring. This is true not only in our own physical body but also in the body of Christ as a whole. If we choose to walk with sin, we leave ourselves and the body of believers exposed, creating footholds for the enemy of our souls. How many years did Jeremiah the prophet speak against God's people choosing to live with the Babylonian gods while ignoring the Lord God Almighty? We think that Babylon was history. We ignore our own selfish materialism and fall prey to the same gods.

We are told, "be self-controlled and alert. Your enemy, the devil, prowls around like a roaring lion looking for someone to devour. Resist him, standing firm in the faith." (1 Peter 5:8-9) We think it does not apply to us. Then we are told, "abide in Me." Yet when such abiding demands obedience, we think again. The commands are meant for shelter and protection. They draw our boundaries in pleasant places, and in so doing, shield us from the storms of sin in our lives.

The wind has tried to fool me into worrying. It speaks with intensity and whistles at high pitches. Gillie barks in an attempt to silence it. Howling back, it laughs at us. Carried mercilessly by the wind, hundreds of raindrops strike the windowpanes with force. They sound like hail. And yet, I know how warm it is outside. The northeastern windows are all rain, making the glass look like a watercolor, the sky dripping into the grey roof and white trim of the house next door and spilling into the silver-grey shingles. A quick break in the sky shows the light of the sun still shining above the clouds. Then it is gone, and another lashing of rain sets in.

Yesterday I was taken up with fear. Fear of losing the warm heat and light in my little cottage. Fear of the giant, impassable puddles that form in the dirt road. Fear of taking the ferry in the storm. Nothing seemed to stop my mind from speculating on future adversity. Paul's success in "taking these thoughts captive to Christ" becomes real when it is your own battle to fight. I am mindful of the encouragement the frightened David found in the caves, "He who dwells in the shelter of the Most High will rest in the shadow of the Almighty. I will say of the Lord, 'He is my refuge and my fortress, my God, in whom I trust.'" (Psalm 91:1-2) And I am also grateful for my friends who close the miles with their prayers.

Walking amidst the elements excites me and keeps my courage high, so I strike out for Pocomo's headlands. Facing the southwest, they are a safe refuge from a northeast wind. Leaving the protection of the car, I nestle Gillie under my jacket, afraid the wind might make her suddenly airborne like a piece of dried seaweed.

Below the cliff, the beach is still, a wonderful silence from the raging of just a few moments ago. The water is perfectly calm. If I had not just wound my way down from the bluff, I would not have believed we were in the midst of a storm. The morning tide has unfurled long rolls of eelgrass along the beach, leaving narrow sand paths between them. Now free from my arms, Gillie takes off running, sand spitting out from her back paws as she races the channels between the eelgrass. These Olympic sprints are abruptly halted by irresistible smells, often precariously tipping her forward on her front paws. Then, nose buried in the sand, she quickly doubles back to trace the trail of the seaworthy remains.

Her usual fare is dead crabs. But it is the combination of her smile, accompanied by the soft crunching of her jaws, that gives her away. She knows the importance of speed and distance. My attempts at confiscating these delights are usually met with a growl, and a fierce look, both of which she and I know are useless, but often give her the time she needs to take the last chomp before quickly swallowing the prize.

We sat upon a wooden stairway to rest about halfway down the beach, my shoulders bumping a Private Way sign hung across the entry. Nestled in the warmth of my jacket, Gillie perches on my lap. Her paws resting on my knees, she keeps her face toward the sea to sniff out its messages. The ferry has just come in. Now a white patch of light amidst the fog, it stands with its mouth wide open, loading up its passengers, a comforting sign that the winds must not be too strong. Maybe tomorrow's journey won't be so bad after all.

A young woman stops to talk with us. She was walking to the inlet at the end of our beach to check the tide for clamming. It seemed a funny day for such a venture. As she spoke,

I noticed that the wind had blown most of her French braid apart. I told her of our findings at the inlet, of the swift-running tide and the layers of seafoam gathering at the shore's edge. The tide was up, and you couldn't cross the inlet to clam. We agreed that timing was crucial for clamming there. I remarked something about my watching and waiting for the ferry and how the ordinary comings and goings of tides and ferries are observed here with simple dignity. I reflected that such simplicity was healing to a world-weary soul.

My friend departed, and I returned to my ferry watch. The front hatch was now shut, and I watched the ferry depart, awaiting its passage by Brant Point and out through the safety of the jetties. At one point, it appeared as though it had stopped. I wondered whether the captain had decided to turn around and go back. I mused about a similar storm during my childhood when our ferry tried to dock at Martha's Vineyard and was blown alongside the dock. After several attempts, the weary captain gave up and went on to Nantucket, much to the chagrin of the Vineyard passengers. Score one for Nantucket.

Slowly the movement of the ferry reappeared. It had merely turned to face the open water. I couldn't see Brant Point in the fog, and I wondered if the ferry passengers remembered to throw their pennies overboard to ensure that they would return to the island. I know I would have been one of them out in the fog and rain.

Thinking of this, I wondered how often we as Christians are willing to obey the Master and head out of our safe harbors into the open sea. I am sure that the captain was not happy about leaving the dock, yet he was called to go. Indeed, we are called to bring the good news of the sun that lies behind the storm clouds, teaching others how to face the storms of life. And whether we like it or not, we carry passengers with us, our families, co-workers, and friends, who trust that we know the way. How difficult a task without Jesus at the helm. Who would ever get on a ferry knowing that the captain had stayed on shore? So why do we think that we can do it without Him?

The ferry is gone. Immediately in front of me, the water is like satin, a smooth deep gray. Yet all around it, wind patterns are playing tag with each other. Occasionally a slight breeze brushes the water, ruffling it as if a school of small fish had suddenly risen to the surface to investigate. The color of the water also changes according to the presence of the wind, as if an invisible hand was pouring in dark ink. And then, in an instant, the wind lifts, and the deep color is gone. Jesus said, "The wind blows wherever it pleases. You hear its sound, but you cannot tell where it comes from or where it is going." (John 3:8)

I rest in His presence. The water directly in front of me is perfectly calm. Touched occasionally by the wind, it remains still, despite the constant activity around it. Perhaps because I have known His presence through the wind at other times in my life, I recognize Him saying, "Let me go before you. I will be your calm just as the cliff behind you protects you and the water from the wind." "When you pass through the waters, I will be with you." (Isaiah 43:2) "And I will stand and protect you through the storms of life. Look now at the calm water before you and remember, I am with you always. Even tomorrow on the ferry, I will go before you and calm the sea. I rule over the surging sea; when its waves mount up, I will be there to still them."

Back at the house, Gillie and I walk to the edge of the beach grass to take one last look at the sea. The waves are pounding the beach as if the sea were trying to spend itself and release its fury. White with foam, the breakers are a stark contrast to the sea's cold green countenance.

The white caps have multiplied as if to mock my faith. I hear the Lord say, "This is the sea that I called Peter out onto." My own voice, filled with the vision in front of me, says, "Oh Lord, how did he do it? How did he step out of that little boat and walk on that water?"

Would I be so bold? I look again at the raging sea, and I am humbled. Peter said, "Lord, if it is you, . . . tell me to come to you on the water." Jesus then said, "Come." (Matthew 14:28-29) Peter believed Jesus and stepped out onto the open water.

Jesus proves himself faithful when I wait or act with the faith He gives me, no matter how small or great. Without action on my part, I would receive an endless stream of faithful acts on His part, but none of them would deepen my own faith. They would be a string of empty gifts. Humbled by the faith Jesus gave him and humbled by the courage he displayed, I pray that I will do Him the honor, like Peter, of using the faith He has given me when called out of my armchair onto the stormy water.

The day of my ferry departure dawned clear and filled with bright sun. While I can hear the waves on the beach, their formidable pounding has left, and there are only small swells on the water. I am thankful for God's faithfulness and for listening to our prayers. The journey across the water will be fine. Just the remains of the storm are evident.

"God is our refuge and strength an ever present help in trouble. Therefore we will not fear, though the earth give way and the mountains fall into the heart of the sea, though its waters roar and foam and the mountains quake with their surging. . . . God is within her, she will not fall; God will help her at break of day."

PSALM 46:1-3, 5

Chapter Eleven

Morning on the Deck

"Morning by morning, O Lord, you hear my voice; morning by morning I lay my requests before you and wait in expectation."

PSALM 5:3

Early morning on the deck. The last scuffs of storm clouds still block the sunrise. The sliver of sky that holds the sun rises golden from the ocean to fill the underbelly of the clouds. The pond is gray, the foam and white caps gone. The sea, however, still pounds the shore, spending the last of the wind and rain.

Gillie is investigating the outer reaches of the deck. Soaked and cool, the pads of her feet probably feel the same touch of fall that mine do. At each boundary, she stretches her head into the *Rosa rugosa* as far as she can without tumbling over the side. Perhaps she is looking for the red hips to eat or is lifting her face to sniff the wind. Her long ears occasionally snare her, and she backs up confused and dismayed, unable even to turn for help. But as usual, I am watching her antics with delight and can effect a quick rescue.

Across from me, a spider has decorated the weathered Adirondack chair with silken strands. Sweeping down the back shoulders to the hand rest, that spider took a daring leap. A gentle breeze now stretches the thin strand connecting the two armrests and pulls it taught like a sail. How strong and delicate is its handiwork. Almost invisible, like the cords that hold me to the Father.

The sun gradually breaks through as the minutes pass, lighting up the houses across the pond and field. I make a hasty retreat inside for my sunglasses and cap. A bumblebee rests on the chair next to me as if grateful for the warmth and dry docking. The birds are out experimenting with the day, floating tiny chirrups on the breeze as if afraid to break into full song. It must have been quite a night for them, wind howling, branches deeply bending, and rain slashing down from the heavens.

They are probably much happier than I to see the sun, besides being anxious to fill their empty bellies.

The goldenrod and tall grasses can now gently sway with the passing breeze, drying out their miniature flowers and leaves, grateful not to be swept full force against each other and pummeled by the rain. Yet despite the battering of wind and rain, the *Rosa rugosa* blooms on, new buds awaiting the sun's full warmth to expose its crown of smiles. Even the privet sports a brighter Kelly green this morning, cleansed of its summer's dust. We needed the rain. I suspect the plants have received it even more gratefully than I have.

In the field below, the brown skeletal crowns of the Queen Anne's lace have survived the storm. Their woody stems are quite sturdy. I know this from my experience of trying to brush one aside while I was watercoloring in the marsh. It persisted in standing upright, despite my efforts to the contrary.

My field of milkweed, however, has most likely taken some damage. Some of the horizontal leaves, bright yellow with the fall, will probably have snapped off. I shall go and see. And hopefully, the pods were wise enough to stay shut last night. The goldfinches will need their silky prize for their long journey home, and the field mice the silk for their nests. Perhaps the yellow leaves will reveal a few hungry goldfinches breakfasting this morning.

I have always loved the morning. Refreshed from sleep, I am relaxed and quiet with the gift of each new day. All of its possibilities lie open before me; fresh hope arises in me like the sun. A new start can be made of anything. I think of Jesus in these early morning hours. The desert, at last, would be cool from the night, and He would find solitude with the Father, knowing full well that in a matter of hours, the crowds would be pressing in on Him again.

After a storm, the stillness of healing and respite from the howling wind comforts my ears. Nowhere does the wind speak so relentlessly as here in a northeaster. But now the storm has melted into the sea, and once again, everything is washed clean, ready to begin anew, happy as the birds flitting among the scrub oak and wild roses.

I am reminded that I, too, have been washed clean. Though my sins were as scarlet, they are now as white as snow. No storm of sin will ever hold sway. For His compassions never fail; they are new every morning. Great is His faithfulness. (Lamentations 3:23 Paraphrase mine)

Like Him, I am comforted by these early morning hours. Abiding in Him is less of a struggle when the rushing about has not yet begun. In solitude, I can dwell in His peace. Morning is the way I would always like to live, quiet, refreshed, breaking light, and cheerful songs.

"When one rules over men in righteousness, when he rules in the fear of God, he is like the light of morning at sunrise on a cloudless morning, like the brightness after rain that brings the grass from the earth."

2 SAMUEL 23:3

Chapter Twelve

Beach Travelers

"'Come, see a man who told me everything I ever did.'"

JOHN 4:29

There is something of ease in a beach walk. And something of friendship in each encounter so freely opened. All of us are travelers on the beach. Absorbed in its beauty and tranquillity, our cares disappear with the first subtle breeze. Our personages are soon made generic.

I think of the conversations I've had while walking on beaches all over the world, and I am struck by how God uses these encounters to do His work. Like puzzle pieces that appear at random, they fit into a larger plan. While I know nothing is haphazard about God's sovereign work, I often cannot see the larger picture. These personal exchanges are a solace for my soul. I hope they serve the same purpose for my new friends.

Today Gillie and I struck upon a beach that would not have been our first choice. The wind was blowing with such force against our intended journey we had to change our course. Sheltered by high cliffs, the northern side of Pocomo affords protection from the southwest winds. The beach that stretches from Wauwinet to Pocomo Point is relatively flat and rocky. Bordered by houses, it is not a usual path for our solitary walks.

A simple hello in passing to a young woman later brought a companionable walk to both of us on her return down the beach. The two of us, satisfied with our solitude for a while, were content to have some conversation. She spoke of her life, her family, and dogs. I talked about my life and Gillie. In the frame of 30-40 minutes, an empty space was filled within me, an answer to prayer. And I suspect in her also by what she said. I know it was more than the setting that tied us. The beach was merely the place to share and link our heart struggles as women. It was soothing to my spirit to find someone, living here, tan and golden, her life finding nourishment from the island as much as mine does. The mainland leaves its scars on us in many different ways, but the sun and sea and clean, soft air have a way of healing the deepest wounds.

In more years than I care to admit, I have fled to this island in search of solace and healing. The excuse was always a vacation, but in fact, my soul was in need of repair. In more recent years, I have returned for physical healing. He has honored all of these inner requests abundantly more than I was able to ask or imagine. His Spirit is so evident here; it is almost palpable. Indeed I live and breathe and find my being here in Him. (Acts 17:28 Paraphrase mine)

I wonder at each one of these encounters what they mean in the overall landscape of God. Whether they are divine appointments. So very often, I walk away wishing that I could have told someone more of the love and care I receive from Jesus. Yet even without speaking of Him directly, I suspect that these encounters are no less important in His plan. I pray that this is so, for that would be a comfort to me. There is no unfinished business in the kingdom of God, even when I go on with my life somewhere else.

I am also grateful for these encounters as I am reminded of Jesus' compassion and interest in every aspect of our lives. I can recall how He always knew precisely what was going on in people's lives, whether it was the Samaritan woman at the well or Zacchaeus in the fig tree. He always knew what they needed and refused to cater to their wants. He knew what was in their hearts.

I do not pretend to have such depth of wisdom, But He is in me, and I have glimpses of His character when a chance encounter touches His Spirit within me. For each time I feel the tug of loneliness, sadness, frustration, or tiredness in another person, I see Jesus showing Himself. And I sense His compassion for these people, for the food and spiritual healing He longs to provide, for the water from which they would never thirst, and the forgiveness of sins that would free them from the world. His gifts along the Way are still available and offered today.

So I cherish these brief encounters, for I believe that it is not only one person I have met, but also two. In every beach walk, the Master is again beside me on the Jericho road, teaching me about His life, showing Himself in each person I encounter, and giving me a glimpse of how far I have walked with Him. Like the woman at the well or Zacchaeus in the tree, He always knows where my heart is.

"As the rain and the snow come down from heaven, and do not return to it without watering the earth and making it bud and flourish, so that it yields seed for the sower and bread for the eater, so is my word that goes out from my mouth: It will not return to me empty, but will accomplish what I desire and achieve the purpose for which I sent it."

ISAIAH 55:10-11

Chapter Thirteen

Solitary Companions

"Yet I am not alone, for my Father is with me."

JOHN 16:32

Writing tends to be a solitary occupation, one in which children and husbands are not readily invited. Thus, many of my days are spent alone, except, of course, for Gillie. She is delighted to curl up on my lap and sleep, interrupting me with no momentous questions or problems and covering my legs like a welcome blanket when the weather turns cold.

Being alone and barring interruptions from family and visitors, I can spend long stretches of time simply sitting and listening or watching the beauty of each day unfold before me. This, of course, is not difficult but rather a pleasant task, and on such days the time passes quickly, like the breezes that run through my open windows. The solitude is barely a concern.

Some days, however, the solitude is not welcoming. Instead, it is harsh and tinged with loneliness, making me fight against it as I write. The cause, I suppose, is that I am here, and they, whoever they are, are off together doing something fun. Yet it is precisely on these days that the Lord, in His gentle kindness, carefully favors me with solitary visitors of my own to encourage me in my endeavors.

My first and most repeated visitor is a very healthy rabbit that lives in the hedgerow and comes to dine on our green grass and clover. I say healthy because rabbits on Nantucket seem to have the world by the tail—what little they have. I dubbed him (or was it her?) the "backyard bunny" because of my father's familiar habit of naming all of the rabbits that ruled our backyard in Sconset. Munching contentedly on the long grass, he seemed immune to my observations.

Gillie, on the other hand, was more than enthralled. Roaring off the deck, she vanished down the brick path, onto the dirt road, and into the brush after him. So quick was she that if the painter next door had not had a bird's-eye view of the event, I would not have known which way she'd gone. As it was, a sea of wild roses, goldenrod, and bayberry stood before me, and for a split second, I felt a small gasp of anxiety escape my throat. Then in her own inimitable way, she emerged, racing back and forth on the neighbor's mown paths, ears flying, focused intent on her face, tracking her prey. The rabbit, long gone into thicker scrub, had high-tailed it down some secret trail where even Gillie could not follow.

One morning I spent some time sketching and painting this rabbit, who was outside the kitchen window nibbling his way through his breakfast while my own got cold. Good choice, said I, the grass is more abundant here within the shade of the privet, and one's escape route from barking dogs is a simple hop instead of a mad dash across the lawn. I watched his every move, the angles of his face, and how he used those great legs to balance his body as he hopped around. Occasionally he would stretch one of his legs or scratch an ear, revealing the snowy white fur of his tail and the underside of his legs—a startling contrast to his mottled back. I wondered about those back legs. They were so much larger than his front paws. Did he get tired of always being hunched forward? How high could he reach if he stood up?

His tail was a marvel. To my amazement, thinking himself safe, he would lower his tail to float horizontally above the ground, a layer of gray on the top for disguise and a puff of white below. And there, of all things, was a slight indentation in his rump, the tail's home when folded up against his body! I thought this rather tidy, both for him and by God his creator.

His face had distinctive markings, especially around his eyes and along the bridge of his nose, giving him a character all his own. One can easily see why Beatrix Potter had such fun creating Peter Rabbit. In the early morning sun, the light shone through his ears, making them glow translucent pink. Even his coat was woven in a pattern of varying brown, cream, and black splashes, not unlike the thickets surrounding the house.

Yesterday my solitude was visited by the wren, or Mrs. Wren, as I have become fond of calling her. As I stretched out in the lounge chair, she came for a visit and perched her tiny feet on the deck, her russet body a warm contrast to the weathered gray boards. Bobbing her tail up and down, she looked around, eyed me closely, chirruped, and flew to the privet. And while she never reappeared so close again, she accompanied me with her songs all day in the thickets beyond the privet hedge. On other days, her happy warbling punctuated my afternoons in various locations. Wherever I was, she seemed to be my constant companion.

One of the most unusual visitors I received was a majestic white swan that appeared one day, gliding across the pond. I spent most of the next three days watching him swim and preen and nap on the beach. I know that swans are often not the most welcome visitors to either humans or other birds. But this one seemed to negotiate a reasonable treaty with the flock of black-back gulls and cormorants that shelter on the spit of sand and wade in the shallows of the channel that refreshes the pond.

I did notice that despite his stately appearance, he approached the shore tentatively, perhaps to sound out the inhabitants before gaining ground. It seemed almost tragic that the other birds did not herald his presence with delight. Especially since he was all alone. Perhaps they were worried about losing their stake on the promontory. Or maybe they were afraid of him.

I am reminded of Christ's entry into Jerusalem, his triumphant arrival on a colt, and His lonely walk to Golgotha. Many stood and watched. Many parted the way for him, shouting hosannas. But others were only interested in stopping Him from interrupting their corner on religion. And He, "the radiance of God's glory," (Hebrews 1:3) also was not received with the welcome He deserved. Like the birds on the spit of sand, we can be threatened and push Him away. We can keep Him at arms' distance. Ultimately, however, if we continue to turn away, our hearts harden, and we will live without Him forever.

I watched this swan for three days, hoping that another of his kind would join him. Perhaps he had lost his mate and was alone and searching for some companionship. Or maybe he'd been thrown out of the regular marsh and was feeling abandoned. I was surprised at the well of my feelings that his presence brought to the surface. Most of them were projections of my own existence and experiences of loneliness and rejection. I am comforted that Christ also knew these feelings. And, just as He cares for the sparrows of the air, He cares for me in every way.

The swan stayed for three days. On the third day, the wind vanished, smoothing the pond's surface to glass. It was pretty remarkable to see him majestically glide across the pond, cutting a perfect "V" in his wake as if to announce victory against the storms of his life.

While I didn't see him disappear on the third day, the

wind kicked up, and I suspect he sought shelter in the marshes on the far side of the pond or some other more peaceful inlet. I enjoyed his company and hope that he is safe. Perhaps he has even found another lonely swan with whom he can spend his days.

Whether by the sea, on the dirt roads, or in my backyard, all of my companions are each an encouragement to me. Regardless of whether they have families or friends, some of the time, they too are alone. I think it more than gracious of my Lord to provide such company for me to make my days just a little brighter with their presence and remind me in yet another way of His abiding presence in my life.

"And surely I will be with you always, to the very end of the age."

MATTHEW 28:20

Chapter Fourteen

His or Mine?

"How many are your works, Oh Lord! In wisdom you made them all; The earth is full of your creatures."

PSALM 104:24

I'm sitting on the warm deck gazing out at the broad expanse of Sesachacha Pond and Sankaty Light. Here in the early morning, I allow the solitude of the day to fill me. Both French doors are open. The outside air pours into the living room. The deck's surface is warm to my feet, and I am reminded of the numerous splinters I have garnered for stubbornly refusing to wear my shoes. In the fall, after the first cold front from Canada visits us, only one door remains open. Soon I will be confined to looking out the windows that line the face of the house.

It has taken me a week to find my rhythm again. Shedding the mainland conventions of makeup and dress, I am like a child again, hair swept back, scrubbed face, yesterday's shorts and T-shirt, shoes abandoned to the closet. Relaxed and rested, I can receive the island's peace and feel a new closeness to the Lord. Touched by His grace each day, my face has welcomed the warm sun, the sweet fragrance of saltspray roses, wild grapes, and the brush of the Holy Spirit in the wind. All that I see reflects Him. Everything He has created responds to His love. Even I cannot help but respond to this love.

The sky has cleared to the azure blue that the storms leave behind. The day, though a new beginning, still leaves reminders of the previous wind and rain. Walking the sheltered edge of the pond, I find leftover seafoam spun by the wind on yesterday's waves. It floats like a down comforter, quietly caressing the battered shore. On the beach, the foam has gathered up tiny sand particles and hardened into fragile skeletons. Pressed against a bed of eelgrass, its gossamer strands have coated a seagull's feather, and it glistens in the sun.

Such creativity of the Master strikes me in its beauty and

delicacy. So much so that it repeatedly confronts me on my beach walks. Yet this perfect beauty is often glaringly contrasted with items of our own making that also have washed ashore. Just today, in the short passage to the pond, I saw a gold net ribbon lying in the sand, a cast-off from someone's birthday package. How harsh and out of place it appeared in the sand. How ugly in comparison with the neighboring gossamer spun over the seagull's wing.

In Genesis, God looked at His creation and said it was good. Nowhere do I find my personal creative efforts anywhere near this "good." I am often struck by my inability to describe or capture the profound beauty displayed around me. My pen cannot find suitable words in the most extensive dictionary that would come even close to conveying the very essence of what God has created. To say in our language, inspired as it was, that it was *good* merely displays how inadequate our language is to fully describe the "depth of the riches of the wisdom and knowledge of God." (Romans 11:33)

While I believe with all my heart that God endowed each of us with gifts of creativity through his divine wisdom, I am painfully confronted with the evidence that we have strayed from cherishing His work. Using these gifts, we have created a world of convenience for ourselves, most of it at the expense of His creation.

The world was given to us to tend and to steward. It was not provided for us to use up and destroy. Plastic bottles, beer cans, pieces of rubber, and glass stare at me amidst the ordinary wash of high tide. Out of place, they create visual discord in the daily painting of sand, pebbles, and seaweed that the ocean so regularly offers from His hand.

I find that this conflict lies within me also. Jesus said, "No one can serve two masters. Either he will hate the one and love the other, or he will be devoted to the one and despise the other. You cannot serve both God and money." (Matthew 6:24) And Paul, always in constant struggle with his flesh, says, "For what I do is, not the good I want to do; no, the evil I do not want to do—this I keep on doing. . . . What a wretched man I am!" (Romans 7:19, 24) I am continually torn between my fleshly nature and the Spirit of Christ that dwells within me. This tearing can be of the most minute nature or absorb most of my life. Regardless of its size, it is always present.

In my own life, I can see the startling contrast between my days spent out on the moors versus downtown. While I am still drawn to wandering around and looking at the enticing shops, it is not what deeply satisfies my soul and spirit. And even if my soul has been temporarily satiated, I did not fill my spirit with the deep refreshment it needs. My spiritual sustenance comes from long walks along the dirt roads, at the edge of ponds, or by the ocean shore. His creation restores and fills the tired spaces of my spirit, providing hope to my soul for the days to come.

All of nature holds His presence. You don't have to search for meaning or beauty. It's perfectly laid out, waiting to be received and enjoyed.

"For by him all things were created: things in heaven and on earth, visible and invisible, whether thrones or powers or rulers or authorities; all things were created by him and for him. He is before all things, and in him all things hold together."

COLOSSIANS 1:16-17

Chapter Fifteen

Friends

"As long as Moses held up his hands, the Israelites were winning, but whenever he lowered his hands, the Amalekites were winning. When Moses' hands grew tired, they took a stone and put it under him and he sat on it. Aaron and Hur held his hands up—one on one side, one on the other—so that his hands remained steady till sunset."

EXODUS 17:11-12

The road to Pocomo runs straight out to the headland, some of it paved. Regardless of the time of year, most of its surface can only be described as a series of washboard ridges and potholes that defy bulldozers and all calculated driving maneuvers around them.

As the wind was blowing out of the northeast, I chose this beach for Gillie. Here she can run freely without getting sand in her eyes, and I don't have to worry about her eating too many dead crabs or other sea mysteries.

On this particular day, we were about three-quarters of the way down the dirt road when we encountered two large Labrador retrievers guarding the entrance to a driveway. On seeing our car, both were overjoyed and proceeded to trot behind us to the headland where we parked the car. Thinking they would lose interest if we didn't break out of our metal house, Gillie and I sat in the car, basking in the warm sunshine.

The one lab, which I nicknamed Aaron, was chocolate; the black I named Hur. The former looked almost like his father was a Rottweiler, his face as long as mine but a whole lot wider and more muscular. Contemplating their friendliness, I opened the car door, convinced that my personal appearance would persuade them to go home. But instead, they were delighted to see us appear, and even more so when they realized that *we* meant one of their own!

I was still suspicious of their friendliness but soon realized that we would be companions on this journey. The initial sniffing and tail encountering over, we set out for our goal, the salt marsh at the end of the beach.

Both labs ran and splashed through the water, clearly enjoying the day and the walk. As we approached the end of the beach, I could see that the tide was rapidly retreating and the marsh edge rimmed with sand. We would be able to walk deep into the marsh and still return before the tide would come back to strand us.

By nature, I am a timid person. Courageous in my intent, I often hold back when I come to set forth. The Lord knows precisely when companionship will spur me on. What I had seen as two hitchhikers disturbing my solitude now provided me with the courage needed to explore the marsh. I crossed the shallow inlet and headed toward its inner recesses, where I had always wanted to go but had wavered in my previous endeavors. Chocolate and black had become my Aaron and Hur, pushing me onward to win the battle over fear and to explore the land I'd promised to see one day when the tide was right. Now was the time.

Perhaps you might wonder what took so much courage. If so, you are probably more adventurous than I am. But be advised, lingering too long in the marsh can leave you with much more of an adventure than you'd bargained for, such as being stranded with no way out but swimming and no one for miles to call for rescue. And even though the ground is often covered with layers of eelgrass, it is riddled with underground tunnels that can collapse at any moment under your feet. Without a trusted guide, even the beach sand can suck your foot down farther than you would like. So there it is. My marsh fears exposed.

The dogs, however, experienced none of these fears. Especially the chocolate. Tearing off into the grass, one minute he would be racing full speed and the next, airborne, as he leaped and pounced into a channel of water. Undaunted, he would chase the black, coaxing him to do the same. But like me, Hur was more interested in beach treasures than in water sports. Occasionally they would end up in the inlet together, playing with each other. More often than not, Hur had cleverly led Aaron to the inlet rather than be coaxed into the muddy channels. Gillie, of course, was focused on sniffing out dead crabs and any other fragrant offering the tide had left for her.

Each time we encountered a sand spit where the water had withdrawn, the labs would gallantly leap ahead, so I always knew where the sand was the soggiest. Deeper and deeper, we went into the marsh. However, having abandoned my binoculars in favor of being lighthearted, I wished I'd made another decision. For as we walked along the marsh edge, the dogs startled into flight numerous herons, cormorants, and several other unidentified, graceful creatures.

One of the main entries into the marsh is a deep channel, which at tidal change, moves swiftly. In previous years, I have seen a sand shark swimming up this channel, searching for his breakfast. Today, however, the channel is shallow, and the dogs are playing in it, the water reaching only up to their bellies. I know that they can swim, having seen Aaron paddling along, biting the water, and snuffling when it got in his nose.

The chocolate lab is having the time of his life along the channel's edge. Here, muddy catacombs have been created by the tide, as if giant earthworms had worked the soil. Every step loosens pieces of mud into the channel. Occasionally he comes too close to the edge and crashes into the water, disturbing the crabs and minnows that I have been quietly watching.

Deep in the marsh, the grasses and sedges are billowing shades of silver, green and russet. A mist of pink spreads throughout the grasses where the sea lavender is growing. Impatient to be on our way, Gillie tugs at the leash while I wipe the sand off my feet after crossing the channel. Once back on the flat beach by the headland, she takes off running at top speed for the eelgrass.

Gillie, the other dogs, and I have become quite chummy by now. I was starting to feel as if we were all part of the same family. So much so that when Hur disappeared, I suddenly became worried. How funny we human beings are. Once, the two of them were pests disturbing my solitude. Now, several hours later, having shared the day's brilliance and joy, I had become their adopted parent and worried about their demise into a swift-flowing marsh eddy.

No sooner had I contemplated going back to look for Hur than I saw him joyfully bounding down the beach toward Aaron. Both dogs had abandoned us for a group of walkers. The dogs ran ahead of us down the beach, leaping and splashing in the water.

At the head of the beach, I stopped to talk with the visitors. They asked me whether the dogs were mine. Having seen me on the beach with them, they assumed we were fast friends. I now wished they were mine. Back at the car, I watched the new beach travelers walk up the dirt road, the dogs following behind them.

Gillie and I stayed to gaze at the Great Point light and across the harbor. Then winding our way home, we stopped amid the road ruts to talk one final time with the travelers. I chided them about having to serve the dogs their dinner. Aaron and Hur were once again far from their driveway guard post but not at all concerned. Apparently, this is part of their daily routine.

I shall never forget this day and the chance to walk deep into the marsh and find the sea lavender, a precious reminder of my mom. But most of all, each time I walk this beach, I will remember how faithful the Master is to me and how He knows exactly when I am lonely or when I am a little hesitant to set out on an adventure He has prepared for me. He alone knows when I need some joy to make my heart and spirit soar again.

Thank you, chocolate and black, for being such faithful and joyful companions on our walk today. Thank you, Aaron and Hur, for holding up my courage, allowing me to receive your gift of friendship and adventure. I hope Gillie and I may one day find you as welcome companions again on our walks into the marsh.

"Have I not commanded you? Be strong and courageous. Do not be terrified; do not be discouraged, for the Lord your God will be with you wherever you go."

JOSHUA 1:9

Chapter Sixteen

Rosa Rugosa — Saltspray Rose

"Consider how the wild flowers grow. They do not labor or spin. Yet I tell you, not even Solomon in all his splendor was dressed like one of these."

LUKE 12:27

R*osa rugosa,* saltspray rose. Fully opened to the sun, its yellow anthers embrace the chatter of the bees. Amidst even the rain and fog, its pink face blooms on. Waiting until just the right moment, it unfurls its pink flags and smiles up at the sky. I'm sure the honeybees tickle its face, and its personality sports a rampage of minute thorns for the curious field mouse. But it is a joyful countenance in my hedge.

How I would like to be like this rose, proudly displaying bud after bud, carrying bright red pips like Christmas beads on my branches from frost to spring. I would wait patiently for each season, without any doubt of its arrival or impatience with its tarrying. Then upon opening, I would thoroughly enjoy the new life it brings, smiling up at my Creator.

The question is, do I joyfully live and whole-heartedly welcome the sweet word of God, like the bees that come to the flowers? Do I enjoy what the Lord gives me to the fullest? I think not. I often leave off after the first bloom and do not know how to enjoy the many seasons of my life. I complain when it's not spring or summer! And, in fact, I do not always enjoy just "being."

Most of God's creation is purposed simply to be. Perhaps the rose has a more straightforward task. I can argue that it is not a sentient, rational being. It has little knowledge of itself. Argue again. It is quite useless. In Him, I will find my life, and that life is being and abiding in Him. I am the one who thinks I need to be *doing.* But note: the bees aren't *doing;* they're simply being what they were created to be and not trying to be or do otherwise. Their very essence is to gather the nectar hiding beneath each flower's anthers. Our essence is to be in Him and do what He has prepared for us ahead of time. Our work is to love our Creator, to believe in Him, and join in His work.

So why can't I just be like the rose? Or like the bees? Why can't I be satisfied with believing and being in Him? The work will take care of itself, just like it does with the bees. Why do I have to confuse the issue in my brain by creating some new idea about doing or creating work that doesn't need to be done and isn't from God?

I don't know. But I do know that the rose and the bees don't ask these questions.

"The grass withers and the flowers fall, but the word of our God stands forever."

ISAIAH 40:8

Chapter Seventeen

4-Wheel Degree

"But we have this treasure in jars of clay to show that this all-surpassing power is from God and not from us. We are hard pressed on every side, but not crushed; perplexed, but not in despair; persecuted, but not abandoned; struck down, but not destroyed."

2 CORINTHIANS 4:7-9

The more equipped we are in Him, the more rugged the terrain. The deeper we search for Him, the more He expects us to trust Him. It is the same whether in joy or trial. He is always there, teaching and guiding us to walk in His realm.

The sun is quietly lingering on the top two roses that bloom in the hedge by the deck. The privet is claiming its last rays on the western side. Across the pond, the hillside spills golden and green washes of blueberry and bayberry toward the beach, illuminated by the afternoon sun.

It has been quite a day for me. Longing to see the island I remembered in my childhood, I rented a Jeep and took off with Gillie to explore the dirt roads in the moors. As a child, I spent many long and happy hours walking along these roads with my parents and the two dogs. Thinking about it now, it amazes me that the underbelly of our car survived those expeditions! We drove through what seemed like bottomless puddles along ridgeback roads with endless snarls of exposed roots and rocks large enough to take our muffler hostage.

Most people, including the woman who rented me the Jeep, wouldn't understand how much I enjoyed today's adventure. For me, it was a time to reflect on the warm memories of the island that I'd shared with my parents and renew old friendships with those special places that form my spiritual relationship with the island. And, at the very least, it turned into a time of testing my courage.

Throughout my life, I have formed visual bonds with outdoor places. The Lord wove these bonds into an umbilical cord between us when all I could see was His creation. Through nature, I acknowledged His presence, supernatural seniority, and remarkable power, but not His love. So I kept my distance. I really didn't want Him to be the master of my life. And I certainly didn't believe that He would be concerned with someone who was just a speck in the universe. Wrong. Yet He pursued me, purposefully seeking a relationship. When I was faithless, He was faithful. (2 Timothy 2:13 Paraphrase) How much of His love I missed during those years when He was more faithful in many ways than my human relationships.

Today I soaked in His beauty like someone who has lived in a dustbin for years. Everywhere Gillie and I went, the world was painted with colors: green, russet, gold, purple, and azure blue. Ponds, fields, kettle holes, and winding, endless dirt roads. Marshes smiling in the breeze. Hawks riding the updrafts.

Deep in the moors, three ponds were carved out by the glacier thousands of years ago. Each is a delight. One my dad named the doughnut pond. A bog surrounds its dry center, and in the rainy season, its rim fills with water. These days, the bog plants are gradually taking over the open water, and the doughnut is barely visible. Climbing up the hill above the pond, my feet feel like I am walking on clouds, the bearberry lending a sponginess underfoot. Once at the top, looking down on the pond, I stretch out on the bed of bearberry, close my eyes, and let the sun fill my face.

In September, the bearberries are bright red. You might even think they were Nantucket's famous cranberries if you didn't know the difference in the leaf configuration and terrain. Bearberries hide deep within the heath as if shy about their color. The cranberries, however, hang proudly on their stalks like Christmas balls, not at all content to take second place to the leaves. We named our cottage "Little Bearberry" to remind us of our pleasant walks in the moors and the way our house nestled snugly in its lot.

From the pond, looking up at the hill, I once could see a large white rock. Now hidden by the bearberry and scrub, I can only find it in my mind's eye. Every so often, I climb the hill just to look for it. Its stability comforted me in Nantucket's changing landscape. Moved there by some ancient glacier, undoubtedly the rock remains, but the years of encroaching scrub have pushed it back into anonymity. The ivory sketch that sits atop my lightship basket attests to its existence. Picnicking at the pond one day, I sketched that hillside and sent it off to be etched onto the ivory that decorates the lightship basket I received for my college graduation. Today, even our picnic spot is covered with blueberry bushes and brambles, but I remember the day and the view just the same.

The second pond is always filled with water. I suppose the deer are grateful for that. They've marked numerous trails down to its edge and bedded down for the night in the lush grasses that line its edges. Today, after the rain, only deer tracks were found on the dirt road before I passed by. Even after fifty years of walking these roads, wild, crooked roots still recklessly grow out of the soil, and large rocks seem to appear continually in the center aisle of the track. Considering that this is an outwash plain and glacial moraine, the rocks should not be such a surprise. But the endless supply of roots always takes me aback.

The water in these ponds is molasses brown. In certain lights, it looks black. But from a distance, it is painted a deep blue reflecting the sky. Today this blue is further set off at the third pond. Ringed with fire, the low bush blueberry has caught the autumn spirit and is making its final display before winter. I stop to take a photo of it, knowing that only my eye can clearly remember that startling beauty.

Driving moor roads is a bit like walking each day with the Lord. Starting on a high open path, the road soon winds into a jungle of scrub oak. Realizing that there is no place to back up or turn around, I steadfastly renew my will to go forward. Usually, this is when the road begins to narrow and look even more like an abandoned track. Now I'm definitely doubting my pluck and wondering whether perseverance will deliver me. Then finally, the road opens up, and I breathe a temporary sigh of relief. Later, as the road closes in again, I immediately begin looking for places to turn off, and the cycle repeats itself.

Sometimes it's the deep puddles that daunt me. What, go through that? I don't know how deep it is. We might have mud up to the floorboard. Nah, they're only puddles, not ponds. Yeah, right. Swoosh, and I am through another one. Backing up is now not even a consideration. Going through them forward is frightening enough!

After a few miles of dense moors and scrub oak forests, the road seems somewhat familiar. I finally reach the high bush blueberries and deep pond, a landmark I know that is close to the macadam road.

Turning west on the Polpis Road, I head for the beach. Because of my summers at Great Point, I have a particular fondness for the dunes. So I have targeted Dionis and Eel Point for my next adventure. Years ago, birding expeditions took our family into this area of beach and dunes. Today, armed with 4-wheel drive, Gillie and I go crashing down the sand road that dips down into the dunes at the very tip of Eel Point.

Committed. That's what we are now. Here I am, the person

who didn't want to try out the 4-wheel drive, sitting amidst the dunes. Stalling for time, I eat my sandwich. I wonder if I can get out of here or if I will have to swallow my pride and beg assistance from some other explorer.

Shifting into gear, we proceed slowly, getting the feel of the Jeep on the sand. Once I become more confident, we lope along but still slow enough not to get mired in deep sand. I'm beginning to wonder if Gillie and I will get seasick with all this motion. Then I remember that rolling bounce along the sand on the way to childhood summers at Great Point. Now I am having fun! I think I could get to like this!

Later on the south shore, I shift into gear again and roar along the dirt roads without fear of their sudden sand eddies. And as the day turns into dusk, I am driving along the long and rutted roads in the Nobadeer and Madequecham valleys. Dusty is right. Gillie and I have received a light covering, and we are sneezing it out of our noses simultaneously.

My pup is a trooper, a great companion in any exploration. Always willing to get out of the car and avoid bouncing for a short while, she stays with me and never runs off. I think she loves the adventure of the beach, dirt roads, and even the spongy bearberry as much as I do.

Our short encounter with the waves at Long Pond beach was fun for her. As she and I rested on the sand, sheltered by the dune, a large wave crept up and startled both of us. Gillie, the ever-vigilant watchdog, perked right up to guard me. Barking at the wave until she was satisfied that it had heeded her warning, she settled down for a nap. The sand was warm and the sun high. We snoozed contentedly.

Some views become a permanent part of your memory.

Like the one atop the mountains in northern Idaho looking down into the lake, forests, and valley below. Or the stars at night in the North Sea. One of my favorites is looking out across the landscape toward Great Point.

Our final stop, therefore, was Altar Rock. As the sun fades into the western sky, I take my binoculars and look out from this high point across the Polpis marshes and beaches of Coatue. A golden glow softens the reeds, and the blue expanse of water is tinged with pink. Beyond, I stretch my gaze and catch that same glow sliding up the western face of the Great Point Light. Following the dunes south, I look for Double Trouble, the driftwood outpost we occupied during my childhood. Its presence somehow provides a sense of continuity in my life, as if some things haven't changed with the winter tides and man's encroachment.

As we traverse the roller coaster dirt track toward the Polpis Road, I am warmed by the memories of the day. Once safely ensconced at home on the couch, I am surprised by the warmth radiating off my face. It, too, has taken on the rosy glow of the sun. Gillie, catching up on the numerous naps that she missed today, is sound asleep in her bed.

It was a good day. I learned to trust. I learned to have more courage. And once more, He has shown me that walking with Him is a beautiful, often challenging, and scary path. Each section on the journey holds a gift from Him in many surprising ways.

"So be careful to do what the Lord your God has commanded you; do not turn aside to the right or to the left. Walk in all the way that the Lord your God has commanded you, so that you may live and prosper and prolong your days in the land that you will possess."

DEUTERONOMY 5:32-33

Chapter Eighteen

The Remnant

"But now, for a brief moment, the Lord our God has been gracious in leaving us a remnant and giving us a firm place in his sanctuary,"

EZRA 9:8

There is always a remnant.

In the desert of our souls, God provides hope that we might know His unfailing love. Nature, His signature, reflects this remnant both in and out of season. In early winter, our expectation of bright green leaves and soon-opened blossoms carries us forward into spring. June's abundance of climbing roses, washing over trellises and rooftops, pours out the summer in a riotous display.

In late September, however, the appearance of a single pink rose poignantly reminds us of the season's end and the coming of winter. Even here, He has set apart a remnant, filled with His life, saved for that final appearance.

The stalwart, yet gentle pink blossom framed against the grey and silver lattice, blooms joyously under its yoke of God. Long past its season, the fragrant flower pushes out its destiny hidden within that tight green bud. Bursting forth into bloom, it courageously yields to the quiet warmth of the September sun. How like the rose we are, clothed in our eternal destiny, responding to His light and warmth. As in triumph, the revelation of that pink character amid the cool autumn breezes robs death once more of its place and reminds us of the hope of His coming.

In autumn or winter, His hand reveals a portion of His faithfulness in each of my walks. Like the tribes of Judah, each portion of the remnant is somewhat different. The rose that blooms in the September sun. The bright blue periwinkle tucked away in December's anonymity on the sheltered hillside behind my cottage. Or the dandelion, that in February, still hugs the ground in its warm sunny spot along the path of my morning walk. Each flower singles out my eye by its color against the waning season, a testimony of hope, a reminder of His provision. It is never too late in a season to receive new life.

Nature reflects His glory. And one day, it will fill all the earth. Each flower is a reminder of that new and final season to come. God chose His Son to bring that hope. And it is our choice, as part of the remnant, to believe both in and out of season, but particularly through the winter seasons of our lives.

"Always be prepared to give an answer to everyone who asks you to give the reason for the hope that you have."

1 PETER 3:15

Chapter Nineteen

Butterfly Wings

"Sun and moon stood still in the heavens at the glint of your flying arrows, at the lightening of your flashing spear."

HABAKKUK 3:11

Every evening just as the sun is setting, a young man appears across the pond, windsurfing. Usually, I first discover his presence by the quick flash of brilliance the sun makes as it catches his sail. Gracefully skimming across the pond, he turns, and the sail, glistening with its coat of water, reflects the sunset. I watch him glide across the pond like a butterfly dancing on the water, his motion fluid and rhythmic, his slender black body held between the wings, his arms extended like antennae. Of course, when he comes too near, the illusion is lost. But once he has turned and gone back across the pond, I can see his butterfly wings again.

The lower portion of the sail is transparent, reminding me of the spherical markings on the base of many butterflies' wings. And like those delicate creatures, whose wings, when poised over a milkweed pod, will flutter with the stiff breeze, the windsurfer's sail ripples when a short puff of ocean wind catches him off guard.

I envy him, pulled along by the wind, wrapped in the rays of the setting sun. I envy the sense of freedom, of weightlessness that he must feel, and the strength of his shoulders that bear the brunt of the pressure to harness the wind. Yet, I don't envy him the murky bottom, the eelgrass, and the cold water when coming about doesn't happen readily or smoothly.

When he is finished, the young man carries his sail up the wooden staircase like an insect, his wings folded into a carrying position on his back. He gradually disappears into the fading light, and then he is gone.

Such is the enchantment of my evenings. The day now lost and closing into night, I am warmed by the thought that if the wind is right, the butterfly will return once more to court the sunset.

"The wind blows wherever it pleases. You hear its sound, but you cannot tell where it comes from or where it is going. So it is with everyone born of the Spirit."

JOHN 3:8

Chapter Twenty

Angels

"After this I saw four angels standing at the four corners of the earth, holding back the four winds of the earth to prevent any wind from blowing on the land or on the sea or on any tree."

REVELATION 7:1

Sometimes when I walk, I forget to look up. So intent about where my feet are going, or so lost in my thoughts, I miss the sky. In some places, however, the sky calls out to me. Its majesty wraps itself around me and lifts me up to meet it. Whether it's the brilliant robin's egg blue that looks so bright it may burst and pour itself down upon me, or a rainbow of blues that shade from the palest whisper of blue to almost black as it stretches into outer space, the sky is a glorious gift that surrounds me.

Today is such a day. And it is by surprise. Often I take my evening walk where the sky is the most expansive, hoping that its presence will overshadow me and my earthly troubles, absorbing them into infinity, never to bother me again. This is when I shed the cares of the day and ask for advice from the Father about how I have handled myself that day. This is when I experience once more the freedom and forgiveness from sin that He intends for us to live in each day.

Gillie and I are walking in the open fields, she with her nose to the ground, I scanning the treetops for hawks. And then it happens. I look up. And above me is a heavenly display, as if someone had forgotten to close the curtain of that invisible realm and left it open for all to see.

Great swirls of clouds, gloriously spun, glowing pink and gold, stretch from the southern to the northern horizon. All around me, a symphony of splendor grows stronger each moment. Sitting on a hillside, I gaze up into the sky and fill myself with the scene above. Two workmen come by. Oblivious to what is going on above, they see me craning my neck upward. Then they, too, look up and are immobilized. "Incredible." they say, "What workmanship." And I reply, "Yes, and I know the

Craftsman." As they disappear, Gillie and I continue to gaze at the sky. The movement of the clouds is almost imperceptible, but their colors are changing like a prism. Even Gillie seems content to sit and stare with me.

Finally, I decide to walk some more and enjoy the view from a higher vantage point. As I get up and look to the north, I am awestruck. There above me is a cloud in the perfect form of an angel, her arms pressed forward in flight, her gown flowing in the wind. And directly facing her is another angel. Then I begin to see what is unfolding. Right before my eyes are the four angels holding back the wind. Perfectly positioned, facing each other as if waiting for the signal, they fill the sky with their majesty. Cloaked with gold and pink, they hold me transfixed. It is almost too much for me to believe.

As I gaze back across the sky, I see that it is completely filled with clouds and golden with the sunset. Varying shades of pink and gold fill the heavens, and there, suspended in the air, are the four angels.

Soon, as with all cloud formations, they disintegrate, and the sun removes itself from the evening sky. But for me, the image is permanently etched in my memory until that day, when the angels will appear, and the kingdom of God comes to earth. Knowing I will see that day is enough for me. For today, I was given a taste of that time to come.

"And he will send his angels with a loud trumpet call,
and they will gather his elect from the four winds,
from one end of the heavens to the other."

MATTHEW 24:31

"You will go out in joy and be led forth in peace; the mountains and hills will burst into song before you, and all the trees of the field will clap their hands. Instead of the thornbush will grow the pine tree, and instead of briers the myrtle will grow. This will be for the Lord's renown, for an everlasting sign, which will not be destroyed."

ISAIAH 55:12-13